THE ULTIMATE BOY BAND QUIZ BOOK

Covering One Direction, Take That, The Wanted, Union J and JLS

Compiled by Chris Cowlin

Unauthorised and Unofficial

First published in 2014 by Apex Publishing Ltd
12A St. John's Road, Clacton on Sea
Essex, CO15 4BP, United Kingdom
www.apexpublishing.co.uk

Please email any queries to Chris Cowlin:
mail@apexpublishing.co.uk

Print layout by
Andrews UK Limited
www.andrewsuk.com

Contents

Questions

One Direction

1. Can you name all of the band members?

2. To which record label did the group sign following The X Factor?

3. In which month during 2011 did the band release their debut single 'What Makes You Beautiful'?

4. Which band member, who was born on Christmas Eve 1991, is the oldest?

5. How many songs are on One Direction's first album (standard album) - 11, 13 or 15?

6. Who is sitting on the left hand side on the cover picture of One Direction's single 'Gotta Be You'?

7. On which ITV television show did One Direction first perform their single 'What Makes You Beautiful' during September 2011?

8. What is the official website of One Direction?

9. What is the title of One Direction's first published book, released in February 2011?

10. In which seaside town did One Direction perform on 19 December 2011?

11. Which band member is Irish?

12. True or false: One Direction made it to The X Factor final in 2010?

13. In which month during 2011 did One Direction make an appearance on Alan Carr's television programme Chatty Man?

14. Which guest X Factor judge suggested that the five teens were put into a band, rather than being five individuals, and qualifying for the groups category?

15. How many weeks did One Direction's single 'Gotta Be You' stay in the UK's top 100 in the charts?

16. True or false: Niall plays the guitar?

17. What football team does Harry support?

18. On which BBC1 television show did One Direction perform their single 'Gotta Be You' on 18 November 2011?

19. True or false: As of 2012, all band members are not married?

20. Can you name the song that is on the B side to One Direction's single 'Gotta Be You'?

21. Which Natalie Imbruglia song did One Direction sing at the judges' houses stage on The X Factor?

22. What colour hair does Zayn have?

23. With which pop group did One Direction perform a medley of 'What Makes You Beautiful' and 'She Makes Me Wanna' during the 2011 X Factor final?

24. Can you name the three writers of the song 'What Makes You Beautiful'?

25. True or false: One Direction's first album includes songs written by Kelly Clarkson and Ed Sheeran?

26. On which series of The X Factor was One Direction part of the show - sixth, seventh or eighth?

27. What football team does Niall support?

28. Which Snow Patrol song did One Direction sing during the semi-final on The X Factor?

29. What is Harry's middle name - Edward, Frankie or Gerard?

30. In which month during 2012 was One Direction's debut album released in the United States and Canada?

31. What colour hair does Harry have?

32. True or false: One Direction released an official calendar for 2012?

33. In One Direction's music video for the single 'Gotta Be You', which band member walks towards a girl and kisses her at the end of the video?

34. What is Liam's middle name - Jay, James or Joseph?

35. True or false: Harry dated Kylie Minogue during 2011?

36. What is Niall's favourite colour - red, green or blue?

37. During One Direction's time on The X Factor, who was their mentor?

38. How many weeks did One Direction's single 'What Makes You Beautiful' stay in the UK's top 5 in the charts?

39. True or false: Harry is related to pop singer Will Young?

40. If Louis had a superpower what would he like it to be?

41. What is the title of One Direction's book, published in September 2011?

42. What was the third song released from One Direction's debut album, released in February 2012?

43. How many times did One Direction play at the HMV Hammersmith Apollo during January 2012?

44. Can you name the three writers of the song 'Tell Me a Lie' on One Direction's debut album?

45. Which Beatles song did One Direction sing during week 7 of the X Factor?

46. What star sign is Harry?

47. Can you name the title of track 11 on One Direction's debut album?

48. True or false: One Direction's first album was the fastest selling debut album in the UK album charts in 2011, selling over 138,000 copies in its first week?

49. Which fellow X Factor contestant did Zayn date for four months, with caused some controversy because of the six year age difference?

50. Which Xtra Factor host was reported to be dating One Direction's Harry late in 2011?

51. In which position in the UK charts did One Direction's debut album peak in the Dutch Albums Chart - 3, 5 or 7?

52. True or false: One Direction appeared at the Princes Theatre in Clacton-on-Sea, Essex, during December 2011?

53. What star sign is Liam?

54. Which band member took part in his school's production of Grease, playing Danny Zuko alongside his girlfriend?

55. True or false: One Direction's first published book reached the number one spot on the Sunday Times Best Seller List?

56. Where in the UK was Zayn born - Bradford, Bury or Birmingham?

57. Which band member during The X Factor bootcamp was nervous when told he had to dance, and remained backstage?

58. Harry has one sister, what is her name?

59. Which band member is on the left hand side of the front of their 2011 debut album cover - Harry, Niall or Zayn?

60. True or false: One Direction's first album was a UK number 1 in the album charts during 2011?

61. In which position did One Direction's album 'Up All Night' peak in the Irish charts during 2011?

62. What football team does Zayn support?

63. True or false: The members of One Direction were appointed ambassadors for Pokémon during 2011?

64. In which month during 2011 was One Direction's debut single first played on BBC Radio 1?

65. How many singles did One Direction sell of their second single 'Gotta Be You' in its first week of release - nearly 60,000, nearly 120,000 or nearly 180,000?

66. How many sisters does Louis have - three, four or five?

67. One Direction finished - second, third or fourth in the 2010 X Factor final?

68. Can you name the title of track 12 on One Direction's debut album?

69. True or false: One Direction's first album was released in Ireland, The Netherlands and Sweden before being released in England in November 2011?

70. Which band member is the youngest, born in February 1994?

71. What star sign is Niall?

72. True or false: One Direction held a concert at Sunderland Football Club during January 2012?

73. What was the name of the charity single that featured The X Factor Finalists 2011, JLS and One Direction, this being a number 1 single?

74. True or false: Liam auditioned for The X Factor in 2008 and made it to the judges' houses?

75. What star sign is Zayn?

76. What is the title of an unofficial biography that was published in July 2011 about One Direction?

77. What is Harry's favourite colour - green, blue or yellow?

78. Which band member is known as 'the joker'?

79. True or false: All band members appeared on a commercial for Coca-Cola in January 2012?

80. What was the name of the song that was a UK number 1 that One Direction was a part of with the other X Factor finalists in 2010?

81. True or false: One Direction broke a record for the most pre-order sales for Sony Music for their debut single 'What Makes You Beautiful'?

82. Where in the USA was One Direction's music video set for their song 'What Makes You Beautiful'?

83. What was the name of the band Harry was in with his friends, performing at weddings and parties, before going on The X Factor?

84. True or false: One Direction sold more than 153,000 copies of their debut single in its first week of release?

85. On which ITV television show did One Direction first perform their single 'Gotta Be You' on 13 November 2011?

86. Can you name the title of track 13 on One Direction's debut album?

87. Which Elton John song did One Direction sing during week 6 of The X Factor?

88. Who wrote the song 'More Than This' on One Direction's debut album?

89. What colour eyes does Liam have?

90. True or false: One Direction's first album was a number 1 in the album charts in Sweden?

91. On which ITV talk show did One Direction appear during April 2011?

92. In which month during 2011 did One Direction release their single 'What Makes You Beautiful' in Germany?

93. What colour eyes does Louis have?

94. Which song did One Direction perform in the 2010 X Factor final with Robbie Williams?

95. What colour camper van was the band in, in their music video for their song 'What Makes You Beautiful'?

96. Where in the UK was Louis born - Devon, Derby or Doncaster?

97. How long is One Direction's single 'What Makes You Beautiful' - 3 minutes 18 seconds, 3 minutes 20 seconds or 3 minutes 22 seconds?

98. True or false: All band members are wearing glasses on the CD cover of their single 'What Makes You Beautiful'?

99. Can you name the song that is on the B side to One Direction's single 'What Makes You Beautiful'?

100. Can you name the title of One Direction's first studio album, released in November 2011?

Take That

101. Can you name the five members of the band?

102. In which month in 2010 did Robbie Williams rejoin the band?

103. Which single did Take That release in October 2010?

104. How many tracks are there on That Take's album 'Progress'?

105. Which Take That song was the first to go to number 1 in the UK charts in 1993?

106. Can you name the two Take That songs that went to number 1 in the charts in 1995?

107. In which year did Take That release their song 'Greatest Day'?

108. Which Take That song won a 2008 BRIT award for 'Best British Single'?

109. Where in the world were Take That when they recorded their album 'Beautiful World'?

110. Which three singles were released from Take That's album 'Nobody Else'?

111. With which female singer did Take That perform their single 'Relight My Fire' in 1993?

112. What colour T-shirts are Gary Barlow and Robbie Williams wearing on the front of their CD cover 'Everything Changes'?

113. Can you name the Take That song that was a cover by the Bee Gees, originally released in 1977?

114. In which year will Howard Donald celebrate his 50th birthday?

115. Where did Take That shoot the video for their song 'I Found Heaven'?

116. How old was Robbie Williams when he joined the band in 1990?

117. True or false: Take That's song 'Could it be Magic' won a 1993 BRIT Award for 'Best British Single'?

118. What is Take That's official website address?

119. In which year during the 1990s did Robbie Williams leave Take That?

120. What is the name of Take That's first album, released in the UK in August 1992?

121. Which single did Take That release in March 2009, peaking at number 14 in the UK charts?

122. What is Mark Owen's middle name - Anthony, Arthur or Albert?

123. True or false: Gary Barlow is a five-time recipient of the Ivor Novello Award and has been voted the greatest British songwriter of all time?

124. How long is Take That's album 'Everything Changes' - 50 minutes 20 seconds, 50 minutes 22 seconds or 50 minutes 24 seconds?

125. True or false: Take That's debut album reached number 2 in the UK album chart and stayed in the UK Top 75 album chart for 73 weeks?

126. Which Virgin Media award did Take That win in 2011?

127. What is Howard Donald's middle name?

128. What is the name of the album that Take That released in November 2009, having recorded it at Wembley Stadium in July 2009?

129. How old was Gary Barlow when he wrote the song 'A Million Love Songs' which Take That released in October 1992?

130. What is the name of the song that appears as track 3 on Take That's album 'Progress'?

131. Who was the producer of Take That's album 'The Circus'?

132. True or false: Robbie Williams supports Port Vale Football Club?

133. Which Take That single was released in June 1992, its highest UK chart position being at number 7?

134. How long is Take That's single 'Rule the World' (the radio edit version) - 3 minutes 54 minutes, 3 minutes 56 seconds or 3 minutes 58 seconds?

135. Which actress did Mark Owen marry in November 2009 in Scotland?

136. How many stars out of five did The Independent newspaper give Take That's album 'Progress' when it was reviewed?

137. Which reality TV show did Mark Owen win the second series of during November 2002?

138. On what date in January does Gary Barlow celebrate his birthday?

139. True or false: In 2007 Howard Donald suffered a collapsed lung after performing a series of gymnastic stunts on stage?

140. What is the name of the song that is on the 'B' side of Take That's single 'Everything Changes'?

141. True or false: Take That's single 'Patience' was a number 1 in the charts in Denmark?

142. What is the name of the Robbie Williams and Gary Barlow's song released in October 2010?

143. True or false: Gary Barlow won The Sun newspaper's 'Lord of the Year' award in 2009?

144. What is Jason Orange's middle name - Thomas, Timothy or Trevor?

145. Which BRIT Award did Take That win in 2011?

146. What is the main colour on Take That's album 'Progress'?

147. What was the best position in the UK charts that Take That's single 'A Million Love Songs' got to?

148. True or false: Mark Owen has had a solo number 1 in his career?

149. What football team does Gary Barlow support?

150. What record label produced Take That's album 'The Circus'?

151. True or false: Take That's album 'Everything Changes' was the third best selling album of 1993 in the UK?

152. What is the name of Howard Donald's two daughters?

153. Which song was on the 'B' side of Take That's 1992 single 'Once You've Tasted Love'?

154. In which year did Take That get together for the ITV documentary Take That: For the Record?

155. Which finalist sang with Take That and performed the group's song 'A Million Love Songs' in the final of The X Factor during December 2006?

156. Which Take That song was made available to download during May 2011?

157. For which Take That song did the group win two BRIT awards in 1994, for Best British Single and Best British Video?

158. What was the title of the song Take That released exclusively for Comic Relief in 2011?

159. True or false: Take That's first ever song 'Do What U Like' released in 1991 peaked at position 82 in the UK charts?

160. At what position in the Italian charts did Take That's 2007 single 'I'd Wait for Life' peak?

161. Which charity was benefitting from Gary Barlow performing his single 'Shame' alongside Robbie Williams at Twickenham Stadium during September 2010?

162. What was the name of Take That's tour which ran from April 1996 until June 1996?

163. Which single did Take That perform live at the BBC for Children in Need during November 2008?

164. Which single was nominated at the iTunes Awards for 'Best Album' in 2010?

165. Which band member once attended South Trafford College in Altrincham, studying psychology, biology, history and sciences at A-Level?

166. What was the name of Mark Owen's first solo single, released in November 1996, the best position in the UK charts being at number 3?

167. Where was Take That's 2007 music video 'Rule the World' filmed, directed by Barney Clay?

168. Which ECHO Award did Take That win in 2011?

169. True or false: Take That won the 2009 BRIT Award for 'Best British Group'?

170. Which song was Take That's first release from their third album?

171. At which football stadium did Take That start their Circus Live tour in June 2009?

172. In 2009, the Sunday Times Rich List claimed Robbie Williams was worth over - £30 million, 80 million or £130 million?

173. True or false: Mark Owen's real Christian name is Donald?

174. Which record label produced Take That's single 'Back for Good'?

175. True or false: Take That's 2007 single 'Rule the World' was a UK number 1?

176. What star sign is Robbie Williams?

177. What was the name of Gary Barlow's first solo single, released in July 1996, this being a UK number 1?

178. Which single was nominated at the iTunes Awards for 'Best Single' in 2010?

179. For which 2011 blockbuster film did Take That record the official single?

180. Which Take That song released in March 1994 features Robbie Williams on lead vocals?

181. In which year did Take That do their first world tour?

182. Which British soul singer was Take That's main support act during their 1996 tour in the UK and Ireland?

183. From which Take That album is the single 'Greatest Day'?

184. For which album was Take That nominated for the 2011 BRIT Award 'Mastercard Album of the Year'?

185. What is the title of Gary Barlow's autobiography?

186. True or false: Take That's single 'Back for Good' won the 'Best British Single' award at the 1996 Brit Awards?

187. Which band member now enjoys playing the guitar onstage, after picking up the instrument for the first time during the making of Take That's 1993 single 'Babe'?

188. In 2004, which band member was inducted into the UK Music Hall of Fame after being voted as the 'Greatest Artist of the 1990s'?

189. True or false: Jason Orange was once a member of the band 'Blur'?

190. What is the name of the record label Gary Barlow founded in 2009?

191. What is the name of Take That's single which was released in February 1993?

192. Which band member took lead vocals on their song 'Mancunian Way'?

193. True or false: Take That's 2007 single 'I'd wait for Life' was their first single to miss the top 10 since their 1992 single 'I Found Heaven', and ended the band's streak of six consecutive number ones?

194. Where did Take That perform their single 'Love Love' for the first time during May 2011?

195. True or false: Take That won the 2009 GQ Men Of The Year Awards for 'Best Band'?

196. In which month during 2009 did Take That release their single 'Said it All'?

197. What is the title of Take That's Compilation album released in November 2005?

198. Who wrote Take That's song 'Love Ain't Here Anymore', released in May 1994?

199. Which record label produced Take That's 1992 single 'I Found Heaven'?

200. True or false: Take That's 1992 song 'Once You've Tasted Love' music video was shot in a warehouse, with the band shown performing the song against a white backdrop?

The Wanted

Band History

201. What was the name of The Wanted's first album, released in October 2010?

202. True or false: The Wanted's debut single 'All Time Low' was a UK number 1?

203. Can you name The Wanted's 2011 single that was a UK number 1?

204. Can you name The Wanted's single that they released in April 2012, peaking at number 2 in the UK charts?

205. How many tracks are there on The Wanted's debut album?

206. Can you name the longest track on The Wanted's debut album, lasting 4 minutes 7 seconds, track 4?

207. In which month during 2011 did The Wanted release their second studio album titled 'Battleground'?

208. Which record company produced The Wanted's album 'Battleground'?

209. How many tracks are there on The Wanted's album 'Battleground' - 9, 11 or 13?

210. In which position did The Wanted's single 'Heart Vacancy' peak in the UK charts?

211. Which rating out of 5 stars did CBBC's Newsround give The Wanted's single 'Lightning'?

212. On which ITV television show did The Wanted perform their single 'Lightning' for the first time during October 2011?

213. In which Spanish island was The Wanted's music video made, for their single 'Glad You Came'?

214. At which venue in Liverpool did The Wanted perform during February 2012?

215. Which music award did The Wanted win at the 'BBC Radio 1 Teen Awards' in 2011 30.

216. What was The Wanted's tour called, which started on 26 March and finished on 15 April 2011?

217. Which The Wanted single was nominated for a BRIT award in 2012 for the 'Best British Single'?

218. Which Arqiva award did The Wanted win in 2011?

219. Which two 4Music Awards did The Wanted win in 2010?

220. Which two Virgin Media Music Awards were The Wanted nominated for in 2010?

221. At which arena did The Wanted appear in Belfast on 8 March 2012?

222. True or false: The Wanted opened and performed at the first Q102's Springle Ball concert during May 2012?

223. Which female pop star did The Wanted support at he concert at the Manchester Evening News Arena on 6 November 2011?

224. Which Canadian pop star did The Wanted support in Brazil on 8 and 9 October 2011?

225. Which music television station broadcast The Wanted's performance at a concert at New York City's Beacon Theatre during June 2012?

226. Which Single did The Wanted release in aid of Comic Relief in 2011?

227. In which year was The Wanted formed?

228. How many weeks did The Wanted's single 'All Time Low' spend at number 1 in the UK charts?

229. How many weeks did The Wanted's single 'All Time Low' spend in the top 100 in the UK singles charts - 29, 30 or 31?

230. How many weeks did The Wanted's album 'Battleground' spend in the top 100 in the UK album charts - 15, 16 or 17?

231. In which position did The Wanted's single 'Warzone' peak, peaking in January 2012 - 21, 31 or 41?

232. In which position did The Wanted's single go straight in at in the UK's singles charts during June 2012?

233. What colour are the words 'The Wanted' on the front of the bands single 'Glad You Came'?

234. True or false: The Wanted appeared and performed at the 2012 T4 on the Beach?

235. Who were the three main guests on 'The Graham Norton Show' on BBC1 when The Wanted performed on the show during 2011?

236. In which month during 2011 were The Wanted guests on ITV morning chat show 'Daybreak'?

237. True or false: The Wanted were musical guests on 'Strictly Come Dancing' during 2011?

238. Can you name two of the five songs that The Wanted co-wrote on their album titled 'The Wanted'?

239. True or false: The Wanted's album titled 'The Wanted' was released in Ireland before the UK in October 2010?

240. Which single did The Wanted perform on 'Sam & Mark's TMi Friday' and 'Alan Carr: Chatty Man'?

241. Which record label produced The Wanted's single 'Lose My Mind'?

242. True or false: The Wanted's single 'Heart Vacancy' was originally written for pop star Leona Lewis?

243. How many stars out of five did Digital Spy give The Wanted's single 'Gold Forever'?

244. True or false: Some of The Wanted's music video for their song 'Gold Forever' was filmed on the same set as the successful film 'The King's Speech'?

245. Who produced The Wanted's single 'Warzone'?

246. True or false: During 2010 and 2011 The Wanted had a number 1 single in USA?

247. True or false: The Wanted performed their single 'All Time Low' on GMTV during 2011?

248. At which arena did The Wanted appear in London on 3 March 2012?

249. At which arena did The Wanted appear in Sheffield on 18 February 2012?

250. True or false: The Wanted's single 'Lightning' was released in Australia and Ireland before the UK in October 2011?

Max George

251. In which year was Max born in Manchester?

252. Which football team does Max support?

253. To which Coronation Street actress was George once engaged?

254. Before getting into music, Max was a football player with which team?

255. With which boy band was Max a member before joining The Wanted?

256. True or false: Max dated Katy Perry during 2012?

257. How tall is Max - 5 foot 8.5 inches, 5 foot 9.5 inches or 5 foot 10.5 inches?

258. True or false: Max appeared in EastEnders during April 2013?

259. In 2008 Max appeared naked on the cover of a British gay magazine 'AXM', in aid of which charity?

260. What is Max's official Twitter address?

Siva Kaneswaran

261. What is Siva's middle name - Michael, Martin or Max?

262. Where in Ireland did Siva grow up?

263. True or false: Siva started modelling at the age of 16?

264. Siva is one of how many siblings - 6, 7 or 8?

265. What is Siva's favourite animal - cat, dog or rat?

266. How tall is Siva?

267. What was Siva's favourite television show when he was a child?

268. What colour eyes does Siva have?

269. What star sign is Siva?

270. True or false: Siva was a contestant on 'Celebrity Big Brother' in 2012?

Jay McGuiness

271. What star sign is Jay?

272. What colour eyes does Jay have - brown, blue or green?

273. In which year was Jay born - 1988, 1989 or 1990?

274. True or false: Jay's real first name is James?

275. How tall is Jay?

276. Where in the UK is Jay's hometown?

277. True or false: Jay was a contestant on Celebrity Big Brother during 2012?

278. What is Jay's middle name - Kelvin, Kevin or Kane?

279. True or false: Jay owns a pet lizard?

280. What colour hair does Jay have?

Tom Parker

281. Where in the UK was Tom born - Birmingham, Bolton or Bristol?

282. True or false: Tom once auditioned for The X Factor but did not get past the first stage of the competition?

283. Can you name Tom's long term dancer girlfriend?

284. True or false: Before Tom joined The Wanted in 2009 he joined a Take That tribute band called 'Take That II' and toured Northern England?

285. What is Tom's official Twitter address?

286. What is Tom's middle name?

287. What football team does Tom support?

288. True or false: Tom learned to play the guitar when he was 16-years-old?

289. What did Tom study at Manchester Metropolitan University, but then later dropped out in pursuit of a professional singing career?

290. In which year was Tom born - 1986, 1987 or 1988?

Nathan Sykes

291. Which football team does Nathan support?

292. True or false: Nathan attended 'The Sylvia Young's Theatre School' from the age of 11?

293. In which year did Nathan attempt to represent the UK in the Junior Eurovision Song Contest which was held in Norway?

294. What star sign is Nathan?

295. What is Nathan's middle name - James, John or Jamie?

296. What is Nathan's favourite colour - red, blue or brown?

297. What pet did Nathan have when he was younger, called Pikachu?

298. True or false: Nathan is known as the baby in the boy band?

299. In which year was Nathan born - 1991, 1992 or 1993?

300. With which British-soul singer did Nathan start a relationship in 2012?

Union J

The Band

301. Can you name the four band members?

302. True or false: Union J is an English band?

303. In what position did Union J finish in The X Factor in 2012 - second, third or fourth?

304. What is the address of Union J's official website?

305. True or false: A book titled The Official Union J 2014 Annual was released in 2013?

306. How many Twitter followers did Union J have at the start of November 2013 - 900,000, 1 million or 1.25 million?

307. In what month during 2013 did Union J release their first album titled 'Union J'?

308. True or false: During 2013 Union J were managed by Gary Barlow?

309. With what record company did Union J sign after their time on The X Factor in 2012?

310. What is Union J's official Twitter name?

Album - Union J

311. In which country was Union J's album 'Union J' released first - Ireland, Portugal or England?

312. On the cover of 'Union J' what are three of the band members sitting on?

313. Which two singles on the album 'Union J' had the band released prior to its release?

314. How many tracks are there on the album 'Union J'?

315. Can you name the title of the song which is track 10 on the album 'Union J'?

316. How many tracks were there on the deluxe edition bonus disc of the album?

317. Which is the longest track on the album 'Union J', lasting exactly four minutes?

318. In what year was the album recorded?

319. Can you name one of the three writers of Union J's song 'Last Goodbye', which is track 4 on the album?

320. Can you name the title of the song which is track 7 on the album 'Union J'?

Tour

321. What was the name of Union J's tour, which started in December 2013 and finished in January 2014?

322. How many of the 20 tour dates did Union J perform in England?

323. In what theatre in Ipswich did Union J perform during their tour in January 2014?

324. In what month during 2013 did tickets for Union J's first tour go on sale?

325. At what venue in London did Union J perform two days before Christmas in 2013?

326. True or false: Union J performed in Liverpool during January 2014 on their tour?

327. Can you name the date that Union J performed at the Blackpool Opera House during their Magazines and TV Screens Tour?

328. At what venue did Union J finish their first tour, on 14 January 2014?

329. Can you name the two bands that were the opening acts during the Magazines and TV Screens Tour for Union J?

330. True or false: Union J performed in Norwich City during January 2014 on their tour?

George Shelley

331. Where in the UK is George from?

332. True or false: George once said he would never date a fan?

333. What is George's middle name - Peter, Paul or Malcolm?

334. True or false: George can sing in Korean?

335. What is George's favourite film?

336. How tall is George - 5 feet 9 inches, 5 feet 10 inches or 5 feet 11 inches?

337. What star sign is George?

338. At the age of 13, George taught himself to play what with some help from his Granddad?

339. What colour eyes does George have - brown, green or blue?

340. What is George's favourite colour?

Television And Video

341. Which single did Union J perform on Britain's Got More Talent during May 2013?

342. On what ITV2 comedy panel show did the band appear as contestants for their Halloween show during 2013?

343. On what British children's entertainment television programme did Union J perform their song 'Beautiful Life' during October 2013?

344. True or false: Union J performed their single 'Beautiful Life' on The Xtra Factor on 27 October 2013?

345. On which ITV women's chat show did Union J perform their single 'Beethoven' on 31 October 2013?

346. True or false: All four band members of Union J were extras in the Halloween episode of the BBC1 soap EastEnders?

347. During what month in 2013 did Union J take over the Daybreak sofa at 7.50 am each morning for a week?

348. True or false: Josh was a contestant on Celebrity Big Brother during 2013?

349. Up to November 2013, how many hits did Union J's music video have for their song 'Carry You' - 5 million, 5.4 million or 5.8 million?

350. True or false: Union J were guests on The Graham Norton Show during May 2013?

Josh Cuthbert

351. Where in England was Josh born in 1992?

352. True or false: Josh's favourite food is an Indian takeaway?

353. What is Josh's favourite film?

354. How tall is Josh - 5 feet 9 inches, 5 feet 10 inches or 5 feet 11 inches?

355. True or false: Josh can squeak his neck?

356. What colour eyes does Josh have?

357. What did Josh do before he joined Union J?

358. Which character did Josh play in his year six school play?

359. How old was Josh when he starred in the West End Musical Chitty Chitty Bang Bang?

360. What is Josh's cat called?

Singles

361. At which position in the UK charts did Union J's single 'Carry You' peak - two, four or six?

362. True or false: Union J released a single titled 'We are Great!' during July 2013?

363. Where in the UK was Union J's music video filmed for their single 'Beautiful Life'?

364. True or false: Union J's single 'Carry You' peaked at number 4 in the charts in Scotland?

365. How long is Union J's single 'Carry You' - 3 minutes 2 seconds, 3 minutes 6 seconds or 3 minutes 10 seconds?

366. In which month during 2013 did Union J release their single 'Beautiful Life'?

367. At which position in the Irish charts did Union J's single 'Beautiful Life' peak - 19, 29 or 39?

368. True or false: Union J's single 'Beautiful Life' was released in Indonesia before it was released in the UK?

369. Where did Union J first perform their single 'Carry You'?

370. At which position in the UK charts did Union J's single 'Beautiful Life' peak - four, six or eight?

JJ Hamblett

371. How tall is JJ?

372. What did JJ do before he became a member of Union J?

373. True or false: JJ was a jockey for around six years?

374. Can you name JJ's girlfriend?

375. What colour eyes does JJ have - dark brown, light brown or blue?

376. Which Take That singer inspired JJ whilst growing up?

377. True or false: JJ has met the Queen?

378. Who is the oldest member of the band - JJ, Josh or George?

379. True or false: JJ is afraid of elastic bands?

380. Which X Factor judge was JJ's favourite?

Pot Luck

381. Which X Factor judge was the band's mentor during 2012?

382. What was Union J called before they changed their name?

383. Which Britney Spears song did George Shelley sing at his X Factor audition, as a solo artist during 2012?

384. Which song did Union J sing during The X Factor live shows, when it was Abba week?

385. Which group had to pull out of The X Factor competition in 2012, creating a spare group slot, meaning Triple J and George Shelley would team up and form Union J?

386. Where in the world did Union J go when they went to the judge's house during The X Factor in 2012?

387. Which Queen song did the band perform during their first live performance on The X Factor in 2012?

388. Which singer did the band beat in week four, in the bottom two showdown, on The X Factor during 2012?

389. Can you name the band's original manager?

390. Which solo male artist won The X Factor the year Union J appeared on the show?

Jaymi Hensley

391. Where did Jaymi first meet Josh?

392. How tall is Jaymi - 5 feet 9 inches, 5 feet 10 inches or 5 feet 11 inches?

393. True or false: Jaymi's favourite food is fajitas?

394. What is Jaymi's favourite film?

395. True or false: Up to November 2013 Jaymi had 17 tattoos?

396. What colour eyes does Jaymi have?

397. Can you name Jaymi's younger brother?

398. What is Jaymi's real first name - John, James or Joshua?

399. True or false: Jaymi can speak French?

400. Where in England was Jaymi born in February 1990?

JLS

401. What does JLS stand for?

402. True or false: JLS used to be called UFO?

403. Can you name all four members of the band?

404. JLS were runners-up on the fifth series of The X Factor in 2008, who won the show?

405. Following JLS's appearances on The X Factor which UK record company did they sign to?

406. Which two BRIT awards did JLS win in 2010?

407. What was the title of JLS's debut album, released in 2009?

408. How many tracks are there on JLS's second album 'Outta This World'?

409. Which pop star featured on JLS's single 'Eyes Wide Shut'?

410. At which number in the charts did JLS's single 'Take a Chance on Me' peak when released in 2011?

411. True or false: All band members are wearing hats on their CD single cover on their debut single 'Beat Again' released in 2009?

412. What is JLS's official website address?

413. Which song is on the B side of JLS's debut single 'Beat Again'?

414. True or false: JLS's 2009 single 'Everybody in Love' was a UK number 1?

415. What is the name of JLS's third studio album, released in November 2011?

416. Can you name the title of track 5 on JLS's third studio album?

417. Which single did JLS release officially release on 1 January 2012?

418. What is the title of JLS's first published book, released in September 2009?

419. Who produced JLS's single 'Take a Chance on Me'?

420. Which JLS single, released in July 2011 debuted at number one on the UK Singles Chart?

421. What star sign is Oritsé?

422. Which other pop band joined JLS and The X Factor finalists to sing 'Wishing on a Star', a charity song, released in 2011?

423. Can you name the title of the single, which was the official single for Children in Need in 2010?

424. Who wrote the song 'Shy of the Cool' which is track 12 on JLS's third album?

425. How many weeks did JLS's single 'Eyes Wide Shut' stay in the UK's top 100 in the charts - 12, 18 or 24?

426. What is Aston's middle name - Iain, Jake or Kelvin?

427. What football team does JB support?

428. How many weeks did 'Beat Again' stay in the top 10 in the UK charts?

429. Where is the band standing on the front of JLS's single 'Love You More' - on the beach, in a lift or on the edge of a cliff?

430. True or false: Marvin appeared in Holby City for three years from 2000 to 2003 playing character Robbie Waring for 14 episodes?

431. How many times did JLS perform at the Manchester MEN Arena on their tour in early 2012?

432. What is Marvin's favourite colour?

433. What are the band members sitting on, on the front of the band's single CD cover 'Take a Chance on Me'?

434. Which JLS album was issued in four exclusive different editions through HMV, each containing a slipcase portraying a different member of the band on the artwork?

435. True or false: Olly Murs supported JLS on tour during the summer of 2011?

436. Which singer from The Saturdays did Marvin start dating in March 2010 and then get engaged to in December 2011?

437. How long is JLS's single 'One Shot' - 3 minutes 30 seconds, 3 minutes 40 seconds or 3 minutes 50 seconds?

438. True or false: Oritsé dated Kylie Minogue during April 2011?

439. When JLS were put through to the final 12 on The X Factor 2008, can you name the other two groups they were put with?

440. Which band member is afraid of big dogs?

441. Which London landmark appears early on in JLS's music video for their single 'Do You Feel What I Feel?'

442. Which two MOBO awards did JLS win in 2009?

443. True or false: Aston entered the television show Stars in their Eyes in 2002 where he appeared as Michael Jackson?

444. Can you name all four judges that appeared on The X Factor during 2008 when JLS were finalists?

445. Which band member is the youngest?

446. How many weeks did 'Everybody in Love' stay in the top 10 in the UK charts?

447. In which country did JLS tour during August 2010?

448. True or false: JLS's debut album was number 1 in the album charts in Ireland?

449. What size shoe does Marvin wear - 8, 9 or 10?

450. What was the name of the book that JLS released in 2010, their second publication?

451. True or false: JLS performed at Tottenham Hotspur's ground White Hart Lane during February 2012?

452. Which JLS album spent 31 weeks in the top 100 of the UK's album charts?

453. True or false: JLS's song 'Superhero', which is on their album 'Outta This World', lasts for 3 minutes 19 seconds?

454. In 2010, JLS signed a record deal in the USA with Jive Records, which song did they release as their debut US single?

455. True or false: Marvin dated Britney Spears for three months during 2009?

456. How old was Aston when he could do the splits?

457. Who is the oldest band member?

458. Which American singer features on JLS's single 'She Makes Me Wanna', released in 2011?

459. Which band member had the nicknames 'Glitzy Ritzy' and 'Music Boy' at school?

460. True or false: Marvin used to be a professional tennis player?

461. What song was the second release from JLS's album 'Outta This World', the single was released during November 2010?

462. Who was JLS's mentor whilst the band was on The X Factor?

463. What was the name of JLS's tour, which they started in March 2012 and finished in April 2012?

464. True or false: When Aston was 14 years old he appeared as an extra on stage with Michael Jackson?

465. In which two months during 2009 was JLS a part of the The X Factor Tour?

466. True or false: JB appeared in Coronation Street during 2007?

467. Which band member is scared of snakes?

468. In which month during 2011 did JLS perform at Norwich City's ground Carrow Road?

469. Which 'Christmas' themed song did JLS sing when they were in The X Factor final in 2008?

470. On which BBC1 show were JLS guests alongside - Robin Williams, Jennifer Saunders and Elijah Wood in 2011?

471. What is Aston's favourite sport?

472. Which band member started the band and found the other members?

473. True or false: JLS performed at the Princes Theatre in Clacton-on-Sea during January 2012?

474. How many weeks did 'Love You More' stay in the top 10 in the UK charts?

475. At which arena did JLS perform on 17 December 2010?

476. True or false: Marvin once worked at Marks and Spencer and Safeway?

477. Can you name two of the five writers of the song 'Go Harder' which is on the band's third studio album?

478. True or false: Marvin is related to pop star Rihanna?

479. What colour car is the band sitting in on the cover of their CD cover of 'The Club Is Alive'?

480. How many weeks did 'One Shot' stay in the top 10 in the UK charts?

481. True or false: JLS were guest judges on The X Factor during the 2011 show?

482. In which year was JLS's third studio album recorded?

483. In November 2011 Aston announced he would be taking part in doing what in 2012 to help raise awareness for Anti-Bullying Week, alongside Pixie Lott and Jedward?

484. What colour eyes does Aston have?

485. True or false: Oritsé has a tattoo with the words 'God, Peace and Love' on his right arm?

486. Which band member has one sister and five brothers?

487. True or false: JLS's debut album spent seven weeks in the top 5 in the album charts?

488. Which JLS music video was nominated for Best Video at the UK Music Video Awards during October 2011?

489. How long is JLS's single 'The Club Is Alive' - 3 minutes 39 seconds, 3 minutes 49 seconds or 3 minutes 59 seconds?

490. What colour is Oritsé's favourite?

491. What Irish band sang a duet with JLS in The X Factor final in 2008 with the song 'Flying Without Wings'?

492. What football team does Marvin support?

493. Can you name one of the two songs JLS sang in The X Factor semi-finals in 2008?

494. True or false: JLS have a condom range with Durex, called 'Just Love Safe', trying to encourage safe sex?

495. Which band member was in his school choir throughout his school years?

496. What star sign is Aston?

497. How many weeks did JLS's single 'The Club is Alive' stay at the number 1 position in the UK charts?

498. What was the name of the hour long documentary on JLS which was shown on television in November 2009?

499. Where in the UK are JLS from?

500. Which boy band released an album titled 'Backstreets Back', this being the first album JB ever purchased?

Answers

One Direction

1.   Niall Horan, Zayn Malik, Liam Payne, Harry Styles and Louis Tomilson

2.   Syco Music

3.   September

4.   Louis Tomilson

5.   13 (the digital version has 15)

6.   Liam Payne

7.   Red or Black?

8.   www.onedirectionmusic.com

9.   One Direction: Forever Young

10.   Southend-on-Sea

11.   Niall Horan

12.   True

13.   July

14.   Nicole Scherzinger

15.   Six

16.   True

17.   Manchester United

18.   Children in Need

19. True

20. Another World

21. Torn

22. Black

23. JLS

24. Rami Yacoub, Carl Falk and Savan Kotecha

25. True

26. Seventh

27. Derby County

28. Chasing Cars

29. Edward

30. March

31. Brown

32. True

33. Zayn Malik

34. James

35. False

36. Green

37. Simon Cowell

38. Four

39. False

40. That he could fly

41. Dare to Dream: Life as One Direction

42. One Thing

43. Two (10 and 11 January)

44. Kelly Clarkson, Tom Meredith and Shep Solomon

45. All You Need Is Love

46. Aquarius

47. Same Mistakes

48. True

49. Rebecca Ferguson

50. Caroline Flack

51. 7

52. False

53. Virgo (born 29 August 1993)

54. Louis

55. True

56. Bradford

57. Zayn

58. Gemma

59. Harry

60. False (It peaked at number 2)

61. Number 2

62. Manchester United

63. True

64. August

65. Nearly 60,000

66. Four

67. Third (Finishing behind runner-up Rebecca Ferguson and winner Matt Cardle)

68. Save You Tonight

69. True (It was released in Ireland, The Netherlands and Sweden three days before)

70. Harry Styles

71. Virgo (born 13 September 1993)

72. False

73. Wishing on a Star

74. True

75. Capricorn (born 12 January 1993)

76. 100% One Direction: The Unofficial Biography

77. Blue

78. Louis

79. False

80. Heroes

81. True

82. Malibu, California

83. White Eskimo

84. True

85. The X Factor

86. Stole My Heart

87. Something About the Way You Look Tonight

88. Jamie Scott

89. Brown

90. True

91. The Alan Titchmarsh Show

92. December

93. Blue

94. She's the One

95. Orange

96. Doncaster

97. 3 minutes 22 seconds

98. False

99. Na Na Na

100. Up All Night

Take That

101. Gary Barlow, Mark Owen, Robbie Williams, Jason Orange and Howard Donald

102. July

103. The Flood

104. 11

105. Pray

106. Back for Good and Never Forget

107. 2008

108. Shine

109. Los Angeles, USA

110. Sure, Back for Good and Never Forget

111. Lulu

112. Blue (light blue)

113. How Deep is your Love

114. 2018

115. Isle of Wight

116. 16

117. True

118. www.takethat.com

119. 1996

120. Take That & Party

121. Up All Night

122. Anthony

123. True

124. 50 minutes 24 seconds

125. True (the album was 'Take That & Party')

126. Best Group

127. Paul

128. The Greatest Day

129. 15

130. Wait

131. John Shanks

132. True

133. It Only Takes a Minute

134. 3 minutes 58 seconds

135. Emma Ferguson

136. Four out of five stars

137. Celebrity Big Brother

138. 20th

139. True

140. Beatles Medley

141. True

142. Shame

143. True

144. Thomas

145. Best British Group

146. Yellow

147. 7

148. False

149. Liverpool

150. Polydor

151. True

152. Grace and Lola

153. Guess Who Tasted Love

154. 2005

155. Leona Lewis

156. Love Love

157. Pray

158. Happy Now

159. True

160. 13

161. Help for Heroes

162. The Ultimate Tour

163. Greatest Day

164. Progress

165. Jason Orange

166. Child

167. Abbey Road Studios

168. Best International Group

169. False

170. Sure

171. Sunderland (Stadium of Light)

172. £130 million

173. False

174. Polydor

175. False: It peaked at number 2

176. Aquarius (his birthday is on 13th February)

177. Forever Love

178. The Flood

179. X-Men: First Class

180. Everything Changes

181. 1996

182. Beverley Knight

183. The Circus

184. Progress

185. My Take

186. True

187. Jason Orange

188. Robbie Williams

189. False

190. Future Records

191. Why Can't I Wake up with You

192. Howard Donald

193. True

194. At the 2011 National Movie Awards

195. True

196. June

197. Never Forget - The Ultimate Collection

198. Gary Barlow

199. Sony Music

200. True

The Wanted

Band History

201. The Wanted

202. True

203. Glad You Came

204. Chasing the Sun

205. 13 (Album titled 'The Wanted')

206. Replace Your Heart

207. November

208. Island Records

209. 11

210. 2

211. 4 out of 5 stars

212. The X Factor

213. Ibiza, Spain

214. Echo Arena

215. Best British Music Act

216. The Behind Bars Tour

217. Glad You Came

218. Best Breakthrough

219. Hottest Boys and Biggest Breakthrough 38.

220. Best Newcomer and Best Group

221. Odyssey Arena

222. True

223. Britney Spears

224. Justin Bieber

225. FUSE

226. Gold Forever

227. 2009

228. 1 (7 August 2010)

229. 31

230. 17

231. 21

232. 2

233. Black

234. True

235. Dame Helen Mirren, Emily Blunt and Ed Bryne 70.

236. July

237. True

238. Say It on the Radio, Golden, Weakness, Behind Bars and A Good Day for Love to Die 76.

239. True (it was released in Ireland 3 days before the UK) 78.

240. Lose My Mind

241. Geffen

242. True

243. 4 out of 5 stars

244. True

245. Harry Sommerdahl

246. False

247. True

248. The O2 Arena

249. Motorpoint Arena

250. True (it was released in Ireland an Australia 2 days before the UK) 100

Max George

251. 1988

252. Manchester City

253. Michelle Keegan

254. Preston North End

255. Avenue

256. False

257. 5 foot 9.5 inches

258. False

259. Cancer Research

260. @MaxTheWanted

Siva Kaneswaran

261. Micheal

262. Dublin

263. True

264. 8

265. Dog

266. 6 foot, 1 inches

267. Buffy the Vampire Slayer

268. Brown

269. Scorpio

270. False

Jay McGuiness

271. Leo

272. Blue

273. 1990

274. True

275. 6 foot, 1 inches

276. Nottingham

277. False

278. Kevin

279. True

280. Brown

Tom Parker

281. Bolton

282. True

283. Kelsey Hardwick

284. True

285. @TomTheWanted

286. Anthony

287. Bolton Wanderers

288. True

289. Geography

290. 1988

Nathan Sykes

291. Manchester United

292. True

293. 2004

294. Aries

295. James

296. Red

297. A rabbit

298. True

299. 1993

300. Dionne Bromfield

Union J

The Band

301. George Shelley, Josh Cuthbert, JJ Hamblett and Jaymi Hensley

302. True

303. Fourth

304. www.unionjofficial.com

305. True

306. 1.25 million

307. October

308. False

309. RCA Records (Sony Music)

310. @UnionJworld

Album – Union J

311. Ireland (on 25 October), it was released three days later in both Portugal and England

312. A sofa

313. 'Carry You' and 'Beautiful Life'

314. 10

315. Skyscraper

316. Four

317. Where Are You Now

318. 2013

319. Simon Katz, Samuel Martin and Matt Squire

320. Where Are You Now

Tour

321. Magazines and TV Screens Tour

322. 17 (two were in Northern Ireland and one in Ireland)

323. Regent Theatre

324. June

325. Hammersmith Apollo

326. True

327. 9 January 2014

328. The O2, Dublin

329. Room 94 and 5Angels

330. False

George Shelley

331. Bristol

332. True

333. Paul

334. True

335. Lords of the Rings

336. 5 feet 10 inches

337. Leo (born 17 July)

338. Guitar

339. Brown

340. Red

Television and Video

341. Carry You

342. Celebrity Juice

343. Friday Download

344. True

345. Loose Women

346. False

347. August

348. False

349. 5.8 million

350. False

Josh Cuthbert

351. Portsmouth

352. True

353. Olympus Has Fallen

354. 5 feet 11 inches

355. True

356. Blue

357. He worked in an office

358. Scrooge

359. 14

360. Oreo

Singles

361. Six

362. False

363. London

364. True

365. 3 minutes 6 seconds

366. October

367. 19

368. True

369. Future Hits Live 2013

370. Eight

JJ Hamblett

371. 5 feet 10 inches

372. He was a model and actor

373. True

374. Caterina Lopez

375. Light brown

376. Robbie Williams

377. True

378. JJ

379. True

380. Louis Walsh

Pot Luck

381. Louis Walsh

382. Triple J

383. Toxic

384. The Winner Takes It All

385. Rough Copy

386. Las Vegas

387. Don't Stop Me Now

388. Ella Henderson

389. Julian White

390. James Arthur

Jaymi Hensley

391. At the Sylvia Young Theatre School

392. 5 feet 11 inches

393. True

394. Avatar

395. True

396. Brown

397. Aaron

398. James

399. True

400. Luton

JLS

401. Jack the Lad Swing

402. True

403. Aston Merrygold, Oritsé Williams, Jonathan Benjamin 'JB' Gill and Marvin Humes

404. Alexandra Burke

405. Epic Records

406. British Breakthrough and British Single for 'Beat Again'

407. JLS

408. 14

409. Tinie Tempah

410. 2

411. False

412. www.jlsofficial.com

413. Umbrella

414. True

415. Jukebox

416. Go Harder

417. Do You Feel What I Feel?

418. Our Story So Far

419. Chris Braide

420. She Makes Me Wanna

421. Sagittarius

422. One Direction

423. Love You More

424. JLS

425. 18

426. Iain

427. Arsenal

428. Five (July-August 2009)

429. On the beach

430. True

431. Two: 30 and 31 March 2012

432. Green

433. Mopeds

434. Jukebox

435. True

436. Rochelle Wiseman

437. 3 minutes 50 seconds

438. False

439. Bad Lashes and Girlband

440. Aston

441. The London Eye

442. Best UK Newcomer and Best Song (for Beat Again)

443. True

444. Simon Cowell, Dannii Minogue, Louis Walsh and Cheryl Cole

445. Aston

446. Three (November 2009)

447. USA

448. True

449. 9

450. Just Between Us: Our Private Diary

451. False

452. Outta This World

453. True

454. Everybody in Love

455. False

456. 11

457. Marvin

458. Dev

459. Oritsé

460. False

461. Love You More

462. Louis Walsh

463. The 4th Dimension 2012 Arena Tour

464. True

465. February and March

466. False

467. JB

468. June

469. Last Christmas

470. The Graham Norton Show

471. Football

472. Oritsé

473. False

474. Three (November and December 2010)

475. Sheffield Arena

476. True

477. JLS, Daniel Davidsen, Jason Gill, Mich Hansen and Ali Tennant

478. False

479. Green

480. Three (February 2010)

481. False

482. 2011 (the same year it was released)

483. To take part in Big March 2012

484. Brown

485. False

486. Aston

487. True (November 2009 to January 2010)

488. Eyes Wide Shut

489. 3 minutes 39 seconds

490. Red

491. Westlife

492. Chelsea

493. 'Umbrella' and 'I'm Already There'

494. True

495. JB

496. Aquarius

497. One (July 2010)

498. JLS Revealed

499. London

500. Backstreet Boys

CPSIA information can be obtained at www.ICGtesting.com
Printed in the USA
LVOW12s2243150714

394465LV00001B/13/P